My First Adventures

MY FIRST TRIP TO THE
LIBRARY

By Katie Kawa

Gareth Stevens
Publishing

Please visit our website, www.garethstevens.com. For a free color catalog of all our high-quality books, call toll free 1-800-542-2595 or fax 1-877-542-2596.

To the JBR Library staff for making my first job so much fun.

Library of Congress Cataloging-in-Publication Data

Kawa, Katie.
My first trip to the library / Katie Kawa.
    p. cm. — (My first adventures)
Includes index.
ISBN 978-1-4339-6251-6 (pbk.)
ISBN 978-1-4339-6252-3 (6-pack)
ISBN 978-1-4339-6249-3 (lib. bdg.)
1. Libraries—Juvenile literature. 2. Librarians—Juvenile literature. 3. Library cards—Juvenile literature. I. Title.
Z665.5.K39 2012
020—dc23

                                    2011024748

First Edition

Published in 2012 by
Gareth Stevens Publishing
111 East 14th Street, Suite 349
New York, NY 10003

Editor: Katie Kawa
Designer: Haley W. Harasymiw

All illustrations by Planman Technologies

Printed in the United States of America

CPSIA compliance information: Batch #CW12GS: For further information contact Gareth Stevens, New York, New York at 1-800-542-2595.

Contents

Today, I am going to the library.

5

It is a place
with lots of books.

7

It lends books to people.

I want to read
about animals.

My mom asks a woman for help. She is called the librarian.

13

She uses a computer.
It helps her find books.

She takes us to a room
for kids. It has lots
of animal books!

My library has
music, too.

I have a library card.
I need it to take
books home.

I love to read!

23

Words to Know

computer

librarian

library card

Index

24